TWILIGHT

How One Man Gave Unity in a Verse to my Universe

KRISH DHANAM

TWILIGHT: How One Man Gave Unity in a Verse to my Universe
Copyright © 2020 by Mala Ministries

Unless otherwise specified, all Scripture is from the NLT.

Mala Ministries
950 W. John Carpenter Frwy
Irving, Texas 75039 USA
www.malaministries.org

7710-T Cherry Park Dr, Ste 224
Houston, TX 77095
(713) 766-4271

Printed in the United States of America

ISBN: 9781648302305

Dedicated To
Zig Ziglar

Mr. Ziglar was my gold standard of someone who walked the talk of Holy writ with admiration for its purpose, application for its people, and adoration for its pursuit. He professed a color-blind God and gave me colorful hope.

He role-modeled Paul and considered me his Timothy. I am grateful to God for the journey of many miles and the fantastic destinations that I took with him. His last words to me were from a moment of fading glory: "Thank you, Lord, for this boy." From the twilight of his own life as the sun was setting on his earthly presence and the heavens were opening up to say, "well done," he once again looked back and reminded me that he loved me and that all he ever saw in me was a child of God. Not black or white. Just twilight. God's incredible moment of uniting day and night.

Thank you, Mr. Z, from your token legal immigrant...
Krish

CONTENTS

INTRODUCTION

Humanity is crying out to God for intervention. The strife on the street is a demand to understand the face of the race. The cry of the heart is to show the face of grace. Like others, I turned to the Word of God to understand the world of God. The solution was not simple, but the signs were significant.

I revisited my journey as a brown man who immigrated to a multi-racial country with a troubled history and turbulent past but was still the world's envy. Accents mocked, stereotypes experienced, and boundaries felt. The weight of disappointment and the fear of debate forced me to be a spectator to life and doubt everything about my situation and surroundings.

I was green with envy about the possibility others had because of their perceived advantages. I was blue with anguish about my lack of preparation and yellow with fear that I could not utilize my potential. My doubt was color-blind. Then one day in January of 1990, I sat in an auditorium and heard a voice of reason. He talked about a color-blind God who created all. He was adamant about standing in front of this God in judgment one day and answering Him.

I found this God later through this very man. Still, in one of his many messages of hope, he quoted Scripture. He stated that since we were all one blood, he was my brother - not a white man with privilege that I believed he had because those were the ones that had colonized my land - but a "brother from another mother," as the folks on the street say. It was not just a statement of connection for this man. It was a statement of conviction. He believed he would be answerable to God because we were, in fact, one blood.

Acts 17:26 was the Scripture and his point of reference.

> *From one man he created all the nations throughout the whole Earth. He decided beforehand when they should rise and fall, and he determined their boundaries.* (Acts 17:26)

He changed his whole life of impact because of one verse. One Man. Whole Earth. Their Boundaries. I was no longer a brown man in a white world. I would be "judged by the content of my character and not the color of my skin," said another man. One Man. Whole Earth. Their Boundaries.

I hope as you read this, you will look up at the God who promises this and investigate the Spirit that fulfills this. We are one blood. One Man. Whole Earth. Their Boundaries. I pray as you read this, you will question your past, qualify your present, and quantify your future, for "He decided beforehand when they should rise and fall, and he determined their boundaries." One God-ordained man, one God-given Earth, and one God-offered boundary.

This book is more a devotional of promise than a description of race and progress. I am not a theologian or a politician; I am just a member of humanity, rescued by others' benevolence, equipped by the wisest teachings, and liberated with the possibility of spreading hope. I hope this book gets more out of you than you will get out of the book.

Krish Dhanam
Flower Mound, Texas

GRATITUDE

For a godly example: My in-laws, Raj Kumar Michael, and the late Maya Michael

For unfiltered and unvarnished love: My bride and son

For helping hands and hearing hearts: My ministry board and the Ziglar family

For gifts of time, talent, and treasure: The many benefactors who support us globally

For belief before the call and benevolence after answering it: The late Paul and Marjory Vickery and Jay and Bettye Rodgers

For spiritual mentoring: The late Ravi Zacharias, Dr. Ramesh Richard, Dr. Jim Ozier, and Dr. Richard Plunk and Ladonna Plunk

For second eyes, better opinions, and more precise expression: Shelley Kurian

For unconditional love and support: My parents, Dr. Dhanam and the late Lakshmi Dhanam

For a constructive critique and loving applause: My American mom Laurie Magers

For encouraging shade and endearing light: Victor Abraham, Brad Huff, Gus Antos, Bill Porter, Kay Hammer, and Sonny Gann

For my forgetfulness and heartfelt apologies: the countless others, who when mentioned, would make these pages longer than the effort

> *From one man he created all the nations throughout the whole Earth. He decided beforehand when they should rise and fall, and he determined their boundaries.* (Acts 17:26)

CHAPTER 1

FROM ONE - OUT OF ONENESS

I have given them the glory you gave me, so they may be one as we are one. (John 17:22)

One day, my job description changed. I was to travel with Mr. Ziglar and be his aide, a salesperson to increase revenue at events where he spoke, and an aide to take care of anything else he needed. He was famous; he was privileged. He flew in front of the plane. He would arrive later, and I would go before him. My job description was to go ahead of him, get the logistics taken care of, and stay behind to finish up all the shipping, handling, and returns.

One day, my job description changed again. "Travel with me. You are too valuable, and God has given me a greater vision for your role. Travel in front of the plane with me. Arrive with me, depart with me, and stay in a hotel room adjacent to mine. You are too important to be working just for my benefit."

But I am not the same as you, I thought. *I have brown skin and none of the pedigree and refinement that goes with your role and responsibility.* Calmly, Mr. Ziglar responded by telling me about the Good Book. We are one blood, and no color can separate us from the will of God. One man was used to replenish the Earth. One man climbed onto a cross and rescued us. John Newton said, "I know that I am a sinner and that Christ is a great Savior."

"That Savior came for my sin, and He has done the same for your sin," he said. "To show you this Man and for you to feel His saving grace and for you to embrace His sacrifice, I need to love you as He loves you."

"How can you love me? How can I be related to you by blood? Why would God's love for you have to transfer to your love for me?"

"I know you have questions, and our time together will reveal many answers. For now, all you need to know is that your past is important because it brought you to where you are, but as crucial as that journey was, your future is going to reveal awe and wonder. You will receive it not because of where you came from and what your ancestors had or held, but because of who you are in Him. One Man.

"Out of His Oneness, we all are united. His shed blood and His spilled blood washes us. One Man. Sit with me, dine with me, travel with me. You are my brother. One Man. Out of Oneness. That is why a great crusader for civil rights wanted judgment to be on character. Character is the ability to have pride in the mundane. The mundane is what we do every day. Sell books and tapes, set up the product table, collect the money. Transfer the goods and ship the product back. You have done a small job with great character and pride. I will give you a bigger job and more visibility. You will be known by the content of your character. Sit with me in front of the plane. You belong, for we are brothers and out of One Man, Oneness."

Prayer:
Dear Lord, may I not see anyone's skin color, but the color of Your blood that was shed for everyone. Let us be encouraged that out of Your Oneness can exist a unity that links us beyond our diversity and allows us to forgive because You first forgave us.

From one man he <u>created all</u> the nations throughout the whole Earth. He decided beforehand when they should rise and fall, and he determined their boundaries. (Acts 17:26)

CHAPTER 2

CREATED ALL - CAME FORTH

God created everything through him, and nothing was created except through him. (John 1:3)

The time is around 10:00 PM. The city is Manila, in the country of the Philippines. I had arrived there three days earlier and carried a burden on my shoulders. My mind riddled with the shame of demotion, and my heart bore the wounds and scars of doubt. I was confident that this might be the last international endeavor on behalf of the organization I represented in no uncertain terms. I had defined them well, I thought. I believed in my heart I had given them my best.

I truly believed that my predicament's only possible reason had to be my race - my color. I was the only one who looked different, acted different, sounded different, and was from another country. When in doubt, it is easy to look at what differentiates us. Satan, the sinister minister of deception, will use anything to make you run to the chapter marked *excuse* in the Book of Life. When misery befalls you, it is harder to investigate the mirror's reflection and believe that He created all. The Great I AM was not on the side of the brown kid. Color mattered. Race mattered. Origin mattered. Origin still matters. He created all, out of one, all.

Mr. Ziglar was arriving at the airport along with his beloved wife, Jean, and another colleague. I chose not to go to the airport to receive them because I was angry. I was lost. I was not his family. They made an example of me because blood is thicker than water. I was water. Mr. Ziglar sent an inquiry to my room as to why I had not been at the airport. I chose to lie. I replied that I was unwell. He knew that I was lying. He told me he loved me and hoped I would get better, as one of the main sessions on goal-setting was to be delivered by me. My only goal was to finish this miserable trip, take my wounds back home, and have a prolonged pity-party.

"He created all" was my reminder again the next morning. *Not me. I am not all. He could not have created me for this situation.* I was innocent. I wanted nothing to do with anyone. I was different, and no one would or could understand me. Mr. Ziglar did understand me. The reason was love and brotherhood. Not defined by daily activity or accomplishment, but a belief in eternal togetherness. He asked me to come up to his room. He knew something was wrong. He sensed my despair. He felt my anxiousness. He was my brother. He knew my wounds because he believed that we came forth from the One who created us all. One who made us all. The One.

I wept and confessed that I had done nothing wrong. "The accusations against me were not true," I pleaded. I felt different. I was brown. Mr. Ziglar looked different. He was white. The One who created us and from whence we came forth was in that room. "Let us pray to the Spirit," said Mr. Ziglar. The Holy Spirit. The One promised as a holy counselor and guide who would never forsake us. He was the solution. He was colorless. He was color-blind.

Mr. Ziglar asked me to call the office, and while he listened to what was an explanation from the company that bore his name, he could hear my muffled sobs coming from around him. An ocean now separated us from where we were and where my guilt or innocence was being judged. "I'm sorry," I kept saying as I cried in front of the man who liberated me. "It's okay, Krish, I love you. I love you," said the man who knew my hopeless chains were mortal, but his love to free me was immortal. He knew the One who created all. Wounds, scars, hopelessness, doubt, and oceans. He created all. He created all.

The time was Holy Week in 1996. Easter in the Philippines. The event was the Born to Win Seminar of the famed Zig Ziglar at the Westin Philippine Plaza overlooking Manila Bay. The seminar was where I would meet the Resurrected One's redeemed glory—the One who created all. I was told to continue and deliver the two-hour goal-setting segment. At the same time, my father in India asked me to perform as if it would be the last time I ever presented a program. Not to do it with the anger of regret, but with the hope of renewal.

I did the best I humanly could, and my earthly hero sat in the front row and watched, listened, and took notes. He cared for me. We were one blood. He told me he loved me. I spoke that day to an audience of one. When I finished, he led my ovation, and the rest who were in that room who trusted him rose with him. As I stepped off the stage, he was there to greet me. He hugged me and told me that he found what he was praying for; that I would be his replacement at the seminar with the same name in the

U.S. Three times a year, I would be given prominence. I would be more than water. I would be like blood. I would understand. He created all.

The report back to the company was delivered with trepidation. "How can we accept Krish? He is damaged goods. We were planning to terminate him. How can he have a prominent fixture in public while representing us?"

Amidst doubt, Lazarus was raised. Amidst non-conformity, Daniel was requested by the kings to interpret dreams. Amidst betrayal, David was called a man after God's own heart. Amidst denial, Peter was told the church would be built on him - the rock. He created all. I was now part of "all."

"You need to trust God," said Mr. Ziglar. "There will be problems in the world, and you will have caused some that will consume you. But He will never leave you. Because He is real to me, and because He created me and created you, I will never leave you. We are one blood. Accept your new role by remembering that you can let your past beat you or teach you."

The One who created all said "come forth" to Lazarus. "Why are you persecuting me?" He asked Paul. "Go, and sin no more," He said to the woman at the well. One Man.

He created all. Like Helen Keller learning a great many new words the day she communicated with Anne Sullivan, I learned, too. I knew that day that I would be asked to come forth with the baggage of despair and accusation and trust Him in life—He who created all.

God allows us to grow and become and move from actuality of doubt to potentiality of promise. But He who created all does not change. He created. He created all. That is why, while we look at the color of our skin and the content of our character, we hope and pray that we can be all He made us to be. Because He says I AM, I can face tomorrow.

Prayer:
Father in heaven, thank You for creating me in Your image. We release our doubts, despairs, and desperations to You to accept Your unique creation for Your divine purpose. Thank You for allowing us to come forth to remind us of Your love, mercy, and hope. Today, remind us to focus on the potential of everyone You created.

> *From one man he created all the nations throughout the <u>whole Earth</u>. He decided beforehand when they should rise and fall, and he determined their boundaries.* (Acts 17:26)

CHAPTER 3

WHOLE EARTH - EVERYTHING

And one called out to another and said, Holy, Holy, Holy, is the Lord of Heaven's armies. The whole Earth is full of His glory. (Isaiah 6:3)

The words spoken by the astronauts aboard Apollo 8 on Christmas Eve, 1968, were from the book of Genesis. Having just witnessed an earthrise from the far side of the moon and unable to give any nomenclature worth its majesty, the astronauts relied on the immortal, timeless, and now timely Word of God. In the beginning. The whole Earth. Everything. In the beginning, God created the heaven and the Earth. One man - God. Created all - entire Earth. Everything.

Lovell, Anders, and Borman were just men, trained to perform, observe, capture, and report. Discover the potential and embrace the possibility. Man would eventually walk on the moon, and a secular society would have bragging rights with lunar supremacy. With its industrial might, the American machine would win the hearts and minds of the world. The sickle and hammer and iron fist of Russian totalitarianism would lose— the whole Earth-everything.

Mr. Ziglar had a picture of an orbiting spacecraft in his hall of memorabilia. A personal inscription from one of those orbiting Earth simply read that his earthly words of motivation and optimism offered hope and guidance even in space. I asked Mr. Ziglar what it was like to have people listening to his messages and embracing his philosophy outside the gravitational pull of the Earth. His response would further simplify the world of God and amplify the Word of God.

"He created the whole Earth and all of us in it. It is not my words that motivate up there," he said, "but the willingness of His people to accept, acknowledge, and applaud His creation." I then remembered my first job description. I remembered moving from the back of the plane to the front of the aircraft. "Sit with me," he said, "eat with me, stay in the hotel room adjacent to mine. You are too valuable in the eyes of the One who created us all."

The prophet said the whole Earth is full of His glory. The astronaut read from the book of Genesis - "In the beginning…" Mr. Ziglar said we are all created equal. All humankind. Why, then, do we have discord amongst humans? Why is there grief and tension in almost every sphere of life? If we are all created equal and have a foundation based on majesty and splendor, why can't we just get along?

Do those who shout and listen even care about what the others think, how they act, and how they feel?

Let me return to the space I call twilight. The part of the day when the morning sun has finished shining its brightest and evening's dusk has settled in anticipation of the night. When created, humanity blushes at its modesty. He created all. He made the setting sun, the rising moon, the twinkling stars, the still clouds, the gentle breeze, and the fragrant seasonal blossoms that emit their heavenly aroma as if on cue. He created all. Why can't man see the beauty of what's around, look at the beauty within, and feel woven into creation? Not as a spectator of angst or an audience of dissent but as a part of the divine symphony. Not black or white, but brown. Twilight.

Rev. Dr. Martin Luther King, Jr. said, "I refuse to accept the view that mankind is so tragically bound to the starless midnight of racism and war that the bright daybreak of peace and brotherhood can never become a reality... I believe that unarmed truth and unconditional love will have the final word." He added that he refused to accept the idea that the "is- ness" of man's present nature makes him morally incapable of reaching up for the eternal "ought-ness" that forever confronts him.

God's ought-ness is the final word. Man's is-ness is the futile world. The last word is all, everything - the whole Earth.

Mr. Ziglar reminded me often of the beauty of God's manifest creation, and how I was designed for accomplishment, engineered for success, and endowed with the seeds of greatness. He made me believe I belonged. I belonged to the whole Earth. I belonged to everything.

Belonging is part of God's story, and believing you belong is part of your role in that story. Your is-ness should always cede to your ought-ness. God has a plan and a purpose for you.

Social constructs emerge in the created world. Physiological and psychological want and desire are byproducts of the world. Liking yourself when someone dislikes you is your ought-ness that is only possible from beyond this world.

"In the beginning" were the astronauts' words when they saw the whole Earth from the moon's far side. "Holy, Holy, Holy," said the prophet when he proclaimed the glory that covered Earth. "I refuse to believe that we are tragically bound to the starless midnight of racism," said Dr. King.

Go back to the beginning, rekindle your ought-ness and reclaim everything—the whole Earth.

Prayer:

Oh, great and merciful God of all creation, show us Your glory. Reveal to us Your purpose for all the Earth that You made. Teach us to love through You and see with You what You intended for us to have because of You. Thank You for everything—the whole Earth.

> *From one man he created all the nations throughout the whole Earth. He <u>decided beforehand</u> when they should rise and fall, and he determined their boundaries.* (Acts 17:26)

CHAPTER 4

DECIDED BEFOREHAND - THAT WHEN IT IS

Afterward, Jesus went up on a mountain and called out the ones he wanted to go with him. And they came to him. (Mark 3:13)

F.W. Boreham, considered one of the most prolific writers of essays, was, in my opinion, the quintessential storyteller of all time. Whether it was coining an apt phrase or interlinking the merger of lives and lanes that leave a legacy, his ability to make prose dance was indeed legendary. Let us ponder his words as we continue to unpack man's oneness as revealed to us in Holy writ.

"A man has not to see another land or another life in order to discover God. Let him stand where he is and scan the ordinary sky with eyes wide open and there blazing brightly above him, he will discover the star, and that will lead him to the life everlasting." F. W. Boreham

The historical facts of racism, prejudice, and bigotry have soiled the hearts of men, condemned and convinced him to participate in that which blasphemes the Spirit of the living God and simultaneously corrupted the soul of the one harboring such ill intent. But God, who made everything, reveals to us that He had decided beforehand the workings of His universe and man's rising and falling. Boreham says that we should not wander to find wonder but stand still and gaze at a single star - and it will lead you to the extraordinary. Jesus just went to the top of the mountain and called on them that He had decided on, and they came to Him.

If the goal and role are decided beforehand, what, then, must we do? How do we know whether we have a prayer, and how do we know if that prayer has us? Can we indeed stand still and gaze in solitary wonder and hope and pray for multiple blessings? But God says that He has decided our rising and falling beforehand. Isn't the Christian worldview supposed to take out the endless abstracts of all the "isms" that permeate culture? Did not the living God say, "I am the way, the truth, and the life, and no man will come to the Father except through me"? If He decided and He stands in the gap, why do we still have prejudice? The answer is to stand still and focus on one star - and it will lead you to everlasting light.

In May of 1995, Suzan Ziglar Witmeyer, the oldest daughter of Mr. Zig Ziglar and Jean Ziglar, was called home to heaven after a difficult illness. The family prayed, the fans prayed, the faithful prayed. She still left them. I was a newcomer to grace and entirely focused on race and did not understand the enormity of love or the enormous burden of grief. In his book, *Confessions of a Grieving Christian,* written to chronicle that time in his life, Mr. Ziglar elaborated that despair was pervasive and personal.

In my view, prejudice is akin to grief in that its application is viewed through personal discomfort, but its resolution must come from public discourse. Even years after a person leaves us, the scars of that wound never fully heal, and at the first sign of similarity, the damage is fresh all over again. The abolition of slavery is global and legal, but the memories surrounding it are embedded in society's very fabric. We attribute grief to losing a loved one or a job, a divorce, an illness, and to lost romantic love in almost the same way we ascribe prejudice to color, origin, demographic, preference, orientation, and linguistics. No matter how collaborative the effort, the individual at the receiving end of it will always feel you don't understand because it is personal. You can choose to look for your shining star and hope it leads to light. You can refuse and look for your parade and hope it clears up your darkness. You can abuse and demand justice, and hope that the world suffocates because you hold your breath. Or you can remember that He decided beforehand. Beforehand He decided.

I remember the compassion of one who chose to show me the light amidst his grief. He shone brighter on his darkest day because he cared for me. He had just buried his daughter and chose to give me a lesson on… beforehand. That's how you remember the lesson as you find yourself at the gravesite, having accepted a pallbearer's role for the coffin that carried your hero's daughter's body. "I know how you feel," I blurted out. I felt I did. He was grieving. We all were. It was somber, and grief was in the air. I actually believed that all I had to do was vocalize my sentiments and share in someone else's suffering. It is like an election where you can participate by way of proxy because you believe the general guidelines are at stake. "You don't know how I feel, son, and remind me to let you know why what you said today would be one amongst the dumbest things you have ever said."

My hero. My superman. My motivator. Mr. Ziglar, my shining star that had pointed me to the light, was correcting me with red-hot rebuke. He had decided beforehand. Beforehand he knew that he would have to rebuke me. A few weeks later, he pointed me to the light again by telling me that I could not imagine or begin to imagine what it is like for a father to bury his child. "How could you know that pain? How can you make that claim? How can you pretend to walk in someone's shoes when you don't know the burden those feet have carried?"

Today, when I look at the claim that everyone makes on their commentary on race, grace, prejudice, and bigotry, I remember Mr. Ziglar's words.

You cannot walk in another's shoes. You cannot tell them you know what it is like to walk in their shoes. Only One knows. Beforehand He knew. Stand outside. Look up. Ask Him. He will become the star that points you to the light.

Thank you, Mr. Ziglar, for the colorful answer. It was pure. It did not look at the color of my skin to teach me. It did not rely on the color of your skin to reach me. It was not the color of anger to preach to me. It was the color of brightness. The brightness that pointed me to the Light Everlasting.

Jesus said to the disciples, "Come to the top of the mountain," because He had decided beforehand. Mr. Ziglar told me that I would never know, and should never say I know, what others experience in grief because he learned early that only One knows.

The One Bright and Morning Star that points to the light. Let us not try to learn to walk in another's shoes, but to take off their shoes, wash their feet and see the scars on their soles that become stars that we can see and follow. Follow them because when we do, we will follow the direction that was known beforehand.

Prayer:
Thank You, Lord, for knowing beforehand that we need the right star to point us to the light. Thank You for giving us Your Son, Jesus, as that Bright Morning Star that can take us from the darkness of our assumptions to the confident conclusion that is the brightness of Your promise. Let us not try to learn to walk in another's shoes, but to take off their shoes, wash their feet and see the scars on their soles that You intend to become stars that we can see and follow.

> *From one man he created all the nations throughout the whole Earth. He decided beforehand <u>when they should</u> rise and fall, and he determined their boundaries.* (Acts 17:26)

CHAPTER 5

WHEN THEY SHOULD - TIME

My future is in your hands. Rescue me from those who hunt me down relentlessly. (Psalm 31:15)

God's timing is perfect. God's timing is precious. God's timing is pristine. He made it all and called it good. Our times are in His hands. He who is outside time sees our past where the gaping holes of doubt try and intersect with the present despair's gnawing suspicion. He knows when they should, how they should, and even if they would. In his conceit, a man wants to mock creation and the difference in the created order and paint a fellow man with an arrogant brush of superiority. Unfortunately, this attitude has led to the curse of bondage during our time. Bondage through shackles of possession and captivity by the subjugation of humanity for all that is vile and indecent.

India, my land of birth, had a caste system amidst a vast populace that was not worthy of a class to look up or down on. Mother Teresa looked upon these forgotten masses cast aside by disease and despondence and said, "Jesus, how could we have left You like this?" Dr. King and Nelson Mandela fought and persevered for another group that suffered persecution for color. God knew when they should. His timing is perfect.

He awoke John Newton from the slumber of enslavement, both as an owner and as a prisoner, and delivered him with amazing grace. William Wilberforce and Abraham Lincoln fought for the emancipation of people all their lives. God knew when they should. Perfect time. Precious time. Pristine time.

Every profession has its Superbowl or World Series. A gathering where the best and brightest would showcase their prowess. For an aspiring speaker, presenting at the massive motivational rallies that crisscrossed America and boasted a lineup of the Who's Who was that zenith and apex. To rub shoulders with those that shaped policy to those that dominated their profession in business, entertainment, academia, and sports, was the ultimate accolade aspiring to be recognized as a communicator. It would be the pinnacle and a platform that could launch careers. I know it did mine. God knew when I should. His timing would be perfect, precious, and pristine.

One such big motivational rally came to Dallas. Two days, two venues, and over 65,000 people in attendance. Dallas was my home turf, and I would finally have bragging rights in my backyard. My family and friends could see and hear for themselves. But alas! The organizers had different plans. I was saddened when they said that they had too many essential speakers scheduled, and the conflict in juggling the precious time of the rich and famous would be enormous. As such, they could allot me only fifteen minutes in the small arena on one of the days.

The others have more influence, I lamented. *After all, I am the only person from India on the program. I am not a former black secretary of state or a white former first lady. I'm just a lowly immigrant. If they could treat anyone indifferently, it would be easier to do so to me.* Perfect time to have another pity-party and lament. It is easy to go down the rabbit hole of doubt and easy to crawl into the hurt's fetal position. But God knew when they should. Perfect timing. Precious timing. Pristine timing.

Enter Mr. Ziglar, the color-blind ambassador of hope who made it his life mission to give me colorful promises. He called the organizers and asked them to take fifteen minutes off his time at each of the venues and allot the same to me. He was willing to give up his limelight so that I could bask in some of it. I have been asked many times whether I was comfortable being in his shadow. Whether I liked being referred to as his token legal immigrant. Whether there was ever a moment of doubt that I was not worthy. The answer is mixed because such moments of doubt are human, and the times you have them are real.

But God's perfect time and precious time and pristine time are a symphony of light. When His divine light shines on the object, you benefit from the shadow. When the object moves, even for a minute, the light falls on you. In Dallas that day, Mr. Ziglar moved. We know God said when they should. God showed what happens when they would. But only God knows the time when they should.

I was allowed in perfect time to stand in front of 65,000 people in Dallas, Texas, over two days. Every one of those people stood when I finished each time slot - each precious fifteen minutes. Each perfect fifteen minutes. Each pristine fifteen minutes. Mr. Ziglar moved so I could have time. God knew when they should, and Mr. Ziglar knew that because God knew, he should. Will you give up your place in the light so that someone else can have the beginning of a shadow they create on their own? Will your ability to lead be anchored in your availability to follow?

If enough people who want to ride away on a high horse of arrogance lean on the carpenter who rode in on a donkey of humility, we will see an ought-ness that surpasses the is-ness. Our content will be full of the character of dreams and not just the color of despair.

He knows when we will rise and fall. From One Man He created all. He orchestrates His symphony. We are just bit players in this symphony. The conductor knows when. The conductor's time is perfect. If you want your time to be perfect, don't focus on today's impatience or the rudeness and indignance of yesterday's importance. He knows when. "He has great plans for you," said the prophet. "Plans to make you prosper and not to harm you."

He knows. Remember - Abraham first rushed God and then in perfect and precious time had Isaac. When it came time for the test, God stopped Abraham from sacrificing his son in perfect time. The sacrifice that is for us is perfect, for He knows when. Remember - everyone who thought they knew met with outcomes that yielded a more significant result that was far from what was expected. Mary and Martha felt Jesus should have come sooner. He knew when the father would be glorified because a greater miracle than healing the sick is raising the dead. Peter wanted to be washed thoroughly, but Jesus knew that the time was perfect just to wash his feet. That way, Peter would realize that the Lord, in His time, did not wash away Peter's ability to deny Him, not once, but three times. He knew that the time was right for Thomas to feel the hole left by a pierced nail so that the doubt of disbelief would be replaced by a voyage of devotion to a land far away.

The seminar promoters wanted to know where they could find the time to accommodate me. Mr. Ziglar knew when I would speak because he knew where he would get the time for me. Pride defines our character in the mundane. The mundane is the passage of temporal time. The habits of hope and the hope of patterns is relying on the divine time. A time so precious. A time so perfect. A time so pristine. He knows when.

Prayer:
Dear God, please unlock the chains of helplessness and hopelessness bound by lies and shackled by unending misery. Let us look to the light that falls on another and learn from and lean on the object that casts a shadow.

When they move, Your light will fall on us in Your perfect and precious time.

From one man he created all the nations throughout the whole Earth. He decided beforehand when they should <u>rise and fall</u>, and he determined their boundaries. (Acts 17:26)

CHAPTER 6

RISE AND FALL - TO SHINE

Now get to your feet! For I have appeared to you to appoint you as my servant and witness. Tell people that you have seen me and tell them what I will show you in the future. (Acts 26:16)

Leadership luminary John Maxwell states that failure is not falling but refusing to learn something while you were down there. G.K. Chesterton concludes that the amount of time spent thinking about a loss determines the amount of time you will need before a win. But the Creator says, "Get up, stand on your feet because it is for this purpose that I have appointed you. Appointed you not only for the things which you have seen but also to things in which I will appear to you."

God says that He knows we will fall, but He insists we rise because of what He will reveal. He asks us to stand because it is in that resilience that His enduring splendor shows. He wants us to shine because He made us out of One Man, called us to a unique purpose, orchestrated our movements and our moods, dictated the time we would need, and designed the moment when He will shine in us, for us, with us, and through us.

The prophet Jeremiah, known as "the weeping prophet," lamented for a nation for forty years and felt lonely carrying his grief. To Jeremiah, the Lord of all creation said, "Long before you came forth, I ordained you a prophet to the nations." As you read this, do you think of the many times you have fallen? Do you remember the many times you rose again? Did you ever look at the journey prophetically and believe that you were ordained to be a prophet to the nations? Did you ever look at how you felt when you were downtrodden and discouraged, and think that there was a God-ordained destiny for you? That you would rise and fall because you can shine? That it would be on the content of your character and not the color of your skin? It would be because He said, "Get up and stand on your feet."

The scene now moves to a city in the Pacific Northwest where I had delivered a two-day training program for a company. The assignment's prestige was one of delight. I was getting ready to shine. The falling was behind me and the rising ahead. No longer would I be judged by my color, separated by my culture, and sidelined for my accent. I would increase, and I would shine.

But God knows that the appointed time and the ordained time were determined before I came forth. My coming and going and falling and rising would be because of my feelings of what I deserved. Yet when questioned by Job, God simply said, "Where were you when I laid the foundations of the earth?" The client's bittersweet scorn replaced the short-lived glory of selection for the engagement. The client demanded the company refund some of the honoraria because they felt I had violated their standards and protocols. *Who are they to criticize me?* I thought. *I am the underdog, and anything I say will act as truth. They are people who live in pristine environments and are surrounded by the best that nature can offer. They know nothing about my immigrant struggles and have never walked a mile in my shoes.* My ignorance was fueled by arrogance, for I believed truly in my heart that a first-generation immigrant in a foreign land had a monopoly on misery. "Where were you when I laid the foundations of the earth?" said God.

If you are reading this because someone gave you this book to provide you with a glimpse into the hope that comes with prayer, then you are at the right part of this text. No one on Earth has a monopoly on plight, grief, misery, or hardship. But everyone on Earth has access to the same prayer and promise. "Arise, get up, stand on your feet; for this purpose, I have appeared to you to appoint you a minister."

When Mr. Ziglar heard of the client's demand for a refund, and when he heard that it was also the policy that I refund his company a portion of my earnings to compensate for my performance, he simply said, "Arise." He reminded me that he was the one who trained me, taught me, prepared me, and sent me. If the client was questioning any of the lessons I offered, they should not just examine the course but also the source. That's why Chesterton also said that you could fall at any angle, but you can only stand in one. To rise and shine because we came from One Man who ordained all the nations and knew beforehand when they would rise and fall takes extraordinary countenance. The countenance that is color-blind in source and colorful in course. Not a blame frame from history but an aim frame from His story.

When you stop looking at life as black or white and start accepting it as twilight, you will see the thread that the great apologist Ravi Zacharias eloquently called "the weave the Grand Weaver weaves." An intricate design that considers the Son's obedience, the father's command, and the eventual tapestry of woven fabric revealing humanity's masterpiece. You are that fabric. Rise and shine. I am that fabric - fall and rise. We are the fabric. Shine.

Relegating our experience to the decision of color and derision of race cheapens existence and humiliates creation. God created the space between day and night as dawn and dusk. The morning's sleepiness is preparation for the wonder of the day ahead, but twilight's majesty is grand design at its finest. The shining of the rising sun begins to fade, and its falling gives way to a dull radiance that prepares humanity for twinkling stars and cosmic scenes of tranquility that let us know that He who made us thought it was good. Twilight is good. "Fall," He said to the sun. "Rise," He said to the stars and the moon. "Before you came forth, I ordained you," He said to the prophet. "I have appeared to you to appoint you as a minister," He said to Saul. "I taught you so I must bear responsibility for what you teach," said Mr. Ziglar.

As a brown man, I was taught by a white man not to see color in creatures, but to see the color in creation. His creation, where He says, "Arise." Looking for the good in others means you depend on the source of your belief always to defend the course of why you believe it. A shallow world focused on superficial skin color will never make a dent in the depth of what God has placed beneath that skin.

Prayer:

Loving God who created the heavens above and the world below, who made the sun rise and fall on command and ushered in day and night as a reminder of Your perfect design, please allow us to look beneath our skin color to the profound depth of Your love. Let us bask in the twilight of Your command to arise and shine and await Your appointment to minister to all Your people.

> *From one man he created all the nations throughout the whole Earth. He decided beforehand when they should rise and fall, and he <u>determined their boundaries.</u>* (Acts 17:26)

CHAPTER 7

THEIR BOUNDARIES — WE WILL INHERIT ALL

I was there when he set the limits of the seas, so they would not spread beyond their boundaries. And when he marked off the Earth's foundations... (Proverbs 8:29)

One of the great joys of the human experience is looking back in fondness at what makes our memories and then looking forward in anticipation for all that is to come. Using the present to work as our crossing between the two is the eternal gift of the One who is the author of time.

When I undertook this short journey to explore the condition of prejudice and bigotry through God's lens, I had to look at my past and wonder where I first saw the seeds of hope. A boundaryless world is utopian, and many modern cultures fight their wars to dismantle any disagreeable boundary. When I first migrated to the west, I appropriated the new culture and eradicated my foundations to participate in something new. The roadblocks can be monumental when you eliminate what defines you and embraces only that which delivers you. Geography, by nature, is designed to have a boundary. It is a place that has borders that foster an identity. God set boundaries on His world as He created it and gave boundaries to those He made to inhabit. Man first experienced shame when he decided that knowledge was more important than fellowship. In that first moment of disobedience, they felt naked and exposed. Human wounds and human scars are the exposed result of rebellion from those self-evident truths that we are all created equal and endowed by a Creator.

Brother is pitted against brother when the fight is to deliver a color or keep it captive. Society launches into civil unrest when those who feel slighted want to slight those they accuse of causing the slight. An eye for an eye of boundaryless lies leaves the whole world blind to God's boundaries. We exist because He said, "I AM." That's the response He gave to Moses when Moses asked who he should say sent him. When removed from a created humanity searching for a solution, the concept of God leaves a void. The psalmist said we were created for His namesake.

To justify the ending of this short excursion, I must take you back to the beginning. The land of my birth. The origin of where I saw a world in which I might belong and a boundary that I would cross to be accepted and acknowledged—a limit made by the Creator who created me and the limitations that would complete my journey. In 2005, I negotiated an agreement with a significant Indian organization that wanted Mr. Ziglar to speak in Delhi's capital city and Mumbai's financial capital (or Bombay, as it was once known). The efforts were tremendous and procuring a favorable schedule from the most in-demand motivational speaker in the world would take almost a year to coordinate.

Mr. Ziglar accommodated all my requests because it was important to me. The boundaries of productivity were being stretched by the boundaryless hope of a man I admired, loved, and respected. "Krish, it is important to you, so let's make it happen." "Krish, I can't wait to get to the land that produced you." "Krish, I can't wait to share the stage with you amongst your people - it will give me the greatest joy!" God's boundaries are the world. Mr. Ziglar's boundaries would now include India. My boundaries would draw a circle over the place whose boundaries I fled to find hope.

But like every moment that has man moving ahead of God, this moment would have misery and memory all rolled into one. Mr. Ziglar wanted me to be showcased alongside him in India, as he had done countless times in other places. I wanted to be beside Mr. Ziglar in India, as I had been in numerous other sites. My bio itself references the fact that I had shared the stage with him more than any other. But India had a boundary they did not want to cross. The white wizard from Texas, USA, was what India's upper echelons would wish to see. To justify his fee, the fee they would, in turn, charge others, would raise the bar of who could afford to attend. They would have to raise the bar of who would be allowed to speak. The little kid from India in Mr. Ziglar's shadow could not be allowed on the program. This was India's boundary. The boundary of inclusion would be selective and exclusive.

I was heartbroken but convinced that if the people in India did not want me to speak on the program, at least they would get the man who had liberated me. Mr. Ziglar would once again establish the boundary of his role as a color-blind ambassador for God. "If Krish does not speak on the program, I am not coming to India." Three commitments conflicted. My commitment to take him to India. His commitment to only speak in India if I could talk on the program. And India's commitment to not have me, but only him. But God, who created all, determined their boundaries. Their boundaries had to include me.

Reluctantly, they gave me an hour on the program while Mr. Ziglar would fulfill the rest of the narrative for the day. I was not on any of the advertising. It was hard to convince those who raised me and taught me that I was also a speaker on that august program advertised quite well. I knew. Mr. Ziglar knew. God already knew. We did two events, and they were received well.

Paul Harvey was known for his catchphrase, "And now you know the rest of the story." Maybe to ensure that you know the rest of the story, I will just tell it to you. At the end of the second event in Mumbai, as the seminar ended; Mr. Ziglar summoned me to stand next to him as he made his final remarks. I audibly remember the exact words that changed me but don't visually remember much else amidst the tears that clouded my sight. "Ladies and gentlemen of India, I came to your country because of how my boy has represented you. His conduct and behavior as an employee, colleague, and brother have always placed this land's culture in high honor. You need to be proud of your native Son. You sent me a scared boy; I bring you back a man who is my legacy." God knew the boundaries He created for me long before I was in my mother's womb. Mr. Ziglar knew the boundaries that I would set for myself. But both knew that to give hope that germinates in creation and gestates in cultivation, we must have boundaries in which we can inherit all.

I have traveled much of the free world since and know that humanity has hopes, dreams, wants, and desires. But to allow a God-sized vision to embrace us, we must rely on the boundaries. Some boundaries will test you, and others will target you, but all boundaries will fortify you.

Prayer:
Lord, let us expand the limiting boundaries and contract the limitless boundaries so that we include Your being as the boundary that defines us in all we do, say, and want. Teach us, O Lord, of those things that we may not get because You know that what You give us in its place is what we need. Thank You, Lord, for the boundaries that You give us to inherit the whole Earth.

MR. ZIGLAR'S OWN WORDS

2-15-99

Dear Krish,

Zig Ziglar

As my friend and "token" immigrant I'm appreciated
your loyalty, ability and sense of humor. You
bring a sense of purpose and a commitment to excellence
that inspires and encourages us all. Your love for our
Lord and for your family is a joy to see. See you
over the top.

Your friend

Zig Ziglar

CONCLUSION

Reader, you may choose not to believe that what God intended for good, man has used for evil in this world. The purveyors of ideological dogma who corrupt the innocent mind of man may choose not to accept any advice from His holy word. But as a recipient of humble grace, pure love, and pure brotherhood, I am grateful for the experience of hurt and healing, scars, and stars. The journeys we take and the justice we seek in those journeys depend more on our response than another's action.

Has man done evil to fellow man in the name of race and religion? Absolutely. Has faith been the last bastion that stood up for the cause of abolition? The stories of William Wilberforce, Dr. Martin Luther King, Jr., and John Newton, say so. But what if you are just a young kid who only hears debilitating news of your past, disappointing evidence of your present, and despondent habits for the future? Do you have a chance to seek out the oneness from whence we came, look at the boundaries of glory available, and acknowledge the rising and the falling of all that is predestined? The answer to me has been yes. The answer to me was to look at the promise of the word that we all came forth from One Man. This verse gives me hope that throughout history, it has been One Man. In the garden, it was Adam. During the flood, it was Noah. For the future, it was Abraham. In the wilderness, it was Moses. Against Goliath, it was David. For wisdom, it was Solomon. For redemption, it was the Christ. For a doubt, it was Thomas. For denial, it was Peter. For emancipation, Wilberforce and Lincoln. For freedom, Gandhi. For deliverance from apartheid, Mandela. For the least of these, Mother Teresa and Graham Staines. For the little brown boy who was not black or white, but twilight, it was Mr. Ziglar.

I hope these pages and principles give you hope and a game plan to look at your journey from the created space of twilight; God's beautiful tapestry drawn every day to see His rising and falling, showing you that His masterpiece is you - marked with the brush of learning, on the canvas of life, with the paint of love.

ABOUT THE AUTHOR

Krish Dhanam, a native of India, migrated to the U.S. in 1986. Winning a sales contest in 1990 earned him a ticket to a seminar conducted by the legendary motivator, Zig Ziglar. Krish joined the Ziglar Corporation in 1991 as a telemarketer and eventually became the Vice President of Ziglar Worldwide.

Krish has successfully delivered his message of hope, humor, and balance in over seventy-five countries on six continents. His client list is the who's who of global enterprise.

Today, he is the CEO of Skylife Success, Global Corporate Adjunct with Ravi Zacharias International Ministries, and President of Mala Ministries. He is the author of *The American Dream from an Indian Heart*, *From Abstracts to Absolutes, Missives, Mottos, and Maxims*, and a contributing author to the book *Top Performance* by Zig Ziglar.

His book, *Hardheaded & Soft Hearted,* was co-authored with Rick Belluzzo, former President of Microsoft.

The Dhanams make their home in Flower Mound, Texas.